EXPLAIN IT TO ME:
WIFI

This publication aims to provide guidance on basic setup and understanding of WIFI technology.

David Laney

EXPLAIN IT TO ME: WIFI

COPYRIGHT © 2024 by Laney & Associates

ISBN: 9798375926735

Eighth Printing 2024:

All rights reserved:

No part of this publication may be reproduced, distributed or transmitted in any form without the written permission from the author or publisher, except as allowed by U.S. copyright law. While care and best efforts have been made to create the contents of this publication, no representations or warranties have been made for the completeness and accuracy of this work.

EXPLAIN IT TO ME: WIFI

Foreword

Writing a publication can be difficult because it requires dedication and hard work.

The process of writing this publication has been a fantastic opportunity for me to discover what I am capable of doing. This writing opportunity has also enabled me to uncover and explore my creativity.

Dedication

I am dedicating this publication to my wife, Darleen, who has always supported me in every endeavor.

EXPLAIN IT TO ME: WIFI

Table of Contents

1. Introduction 5
2. Why should we understand WIFI? 6
3. What is the History behind WIFI? 7
4. What are the Benefits of WIFI? 8
5. What exactly is WIFI? 10
6. What is the difference between WIFI and LIFI? 12
7. What is the difference between WIFI and Bluetooth? 14
8. What are the benefits & cost savings of setting up a WIFI network? 15
9. What do I need to know before setting up a WIFI network? 17
10. What top technologies do I need to consider for a WIFI network? 18
11. How does Speed & Latency impact WIFI? 20
12. How does Security impact WIFI? 22
13. How do I set up a WIFI network? 23
14. What is the Internet modem & what does it have to do with WIFI? 24
15. What is the Router & what does it have to do with WIFI? 26
16. What is a Firewall or VPN & what does it have to do with WIFI? 31
17. What is a Switch & what does it have to do with WIFI? 32
18. What is an Access Point & what does it have to do with WIFI? 33
19. What do NIC cards have to do with WIFI? 34
20. What do Streaming devices have to do with WIFI? 35
21. How do I connect devices to the WIFI network? 36
22. How do I make a software connection to a WIFI network? 38
23. How do I troubleshoot problems with a WIFI network? 39
24. Definitions 41
25. Conclusion 45
26. Credits 47
27. Notes 48

EXPLAIN IT TO ME: WIFI

1. Introduction

This publication is designed to help readers understand the basics of **WIFI,** the **IEEE** 802.11 protocol for devices operating in the 2.4 GHz, 5 GHz, and 6 GHz bandwidths.

It begins by addressing what you need to know before setting up a network, leading technologies to consider, and more.

This publication also covers the basics of Internet modems, routers, switches, access points, VPNs, Hotspots and NIC cards so that you will have all the information you need to get started.

EXPLAIN IT TO ME: WIFI

2. Why should we understand WIFI?

First, understanding **WIFI**, sometimes written as **Wi-Fi**, can help you protect yourself and your data when using public networks. Most public networks are not secure, meaning people with malicious intent can intercept your data. Knowing WIFI and how it works can help you take the appropriate steps to protect yourself.

Second, understanding WIFI can help you troubleshoot problems with your home network. Common issues include slow speeds, dropped connections, and spotty coverage. Knowing the basics of WIFI can help you identify the problem and take the steps necessary to resolve it.

Third, understanding WIFI can help you make the best purchasing decision regarding wireless routers, access points, and other wireless devices. This will allow you to evaluate the options available and ensure you get the best product for your needs.

Unfortunately, many people are confused by the technical terminology associated with WIFI. Terms like WIFI, **802.11** standards, **WPA**, **WPA2**, **WPA3**, and **SSID** can be challenging to understand. It is essential to take the time to understand the basics of WIFI so you can make informed decisions and protect yourself.

Various online resources are available to help you learn the basics. Please note that many words and Terms that have been **highlighted** are also defined in the "Definition" section near the back of this publication.

Finally, taking the time to understand WIFI can be beneficial in the long run.

EXPLAIN IT TO ME: WIFI

3: What is the History behind WIFI?

The development of wireless internet, or WIFI, has revolutionized how we use technology in today's world.

It has made accessing the internet more accessible and more convenient, allowing us to stay connected no matter where we are. But the history of WIFI is fascinating, full of innovative ideas and noteworthy advancements.

In the late 1980s, a group of engineers from the CSIRO (Commonwealth Scientific and Industrial Research Organization) in Australia was working on a project that would later become known as WIFI. The team, led by John O'Sullivan, was trying to find a way to connect computers wirelessly so that people could access the internet without having to physically plug in an **Ethernet (or "category" cat 6, cat 7)** cable. After much experimentation and research, the team eventually developed a system that allowed radio signals to carry data between computers.

This system was the first iteration of WIFI technology. In 1997, the Institute of Electrical and Electronics Engineers (IEEE) created a WIFI standard, 802.11. This allowed for the development of WIFI networks, allowing multiple computers to connect without the need for cables.

This was a significant step forward in the development of WIFI, as it allowed for the use of WIFI in public places, such as coffee shops and airports. In the 2000s, WIFI technology continued to evolve. The introduction of WIFI routers, which allowed multiple devices to connect to a single WIFI network, made WIFI even more accessible.

New technologies, such as **WPA2 or WPA3** encryption, made WIFI networks even more secure. The development of WIFI has had an enormous impact on our lives. It has also made our lives more convenient no matter where we are.

The development of WIFI is an important part of our technological history and one that we should all be grateful for. Without WIFI, the world would be a much different place.

So, the next time you connect to your WIFI network, take a moment to appreciate the innovation and hard work that has made it possible.

EXPLAIN IT TO ME: WIFI

4. What are the Benefits of WIFI?

WIFI is a technology that has become an integral part of our lives. It has enabled us to stay connected to the world without needing physical cables or wires. With WIFI, we can access the internet from virtually any location, whether it's from our home, office, or even on the go.

At home, WIFI is essential for providing an easy and reliable way to stay connected. With it, we can stream movies, access favorite websites, share photos and videos, and stay connected with friends and family. It also allows us to keep track of our work emails and collaborate with our colleagues, even while we're away from the office.

At work, WIFI is essential to keep employees connected and productive. It allows employees to access important documents and work materials, collaborate with colleagues, and stay updated with the latest news and information. It also allows employers to monitor employee activity and ensure that their employees are working productively and safely.

On the go, WIFI is essential for staying connected. With it, we can access the internet from almost any location, including coffee shops, airports, and public parks. We can use it to stay in touch with friends and family, check our emails, and access our favorite websites. It is also helpful for business travelers who need to stay connected and work while away from their office.

Overall, WIFI is an invaluable technology that has changed how we live, work, and stay connected. It provides an easy and reliable way to access the internet from almost any location, and it is essential for staying productive and connected at home and work. Setting up your own WIFI network can be a great way to stay in contact with family and friends.

The pros of setting up your own WIFI network are numerous. First and foremost, you'll be free to control what you allow on your network. You can choose which devices can access the network and which websites or applications can be used. This helps protect your network from malicious activities and viruses and keep your private data secure.

In addition, setting up your own WIFI network can be cheaper than renting one from an internet service provider. You'll be able to save money on monthly fees and the cost of the router, modem, and other equipment. You'll also have more control over your connection speed, as you can adjust the settings to get the best performance from your internet connection.

Finally, setting up your own WIFI network can be more reliable than a public network. You won't have to worry about others taking up your bandwidth or slowing down your connection. You'll also be able to keep a better eye on your wireless network, as you can monitor and adjust the settings as needed.

EXPLAIN IT TO ME: WIFI

However, there are also some drawbacks to setting up your own WIFI network. First, you'll need to ensure you have the right equipment and know how to set it up properly. You'll also need to be aware of local regulations or restrictions, as some areas may not allow specific types of networks.

In addition, setting up a WIFI network can be more expensive than renting one from an internet service provider. As you may need to purchase the necessary hardware and software, as well as have the router and modem professionally installed. Finally, you'll need to be comfortable troubleshooting any issues.

If you're not tech-savvy, you may find it difficult to troubleshoot any problems with your network. Overall, setting up your own WIFI network can be a great way to stay connected with your family and friends. However, it's essential to weigh the pros and cons before deciding. Make sure you understand the costs involved and the risks of setting up your own network.

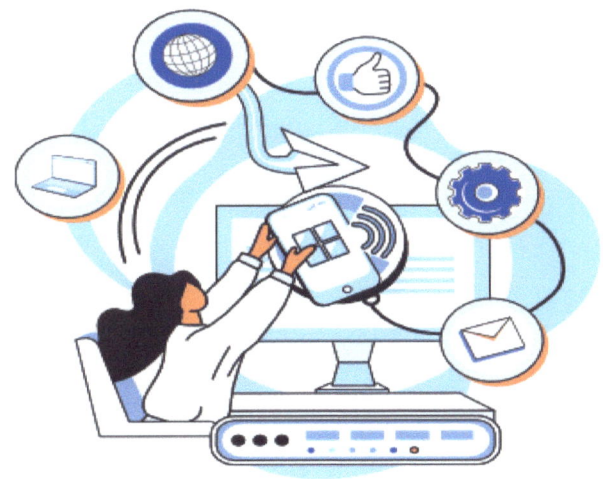

EXPLAIN IT TO ME: WIFI

5. What exactly is WIFI?

WIFI is a technology that allows an electronic device (i.e., *Cell phones, Computers, Televisions, or Streaming devices*) to exchange data or connect to the internet wirelessly using radio waves and is a term used to describe a wireless local area network (WLAN), a type of network that allows devices to connect to the Internet wirelessly. For a more in-depth knowledge of how the Internet works, please reference the publication "**Explain It To Me: Internet**".

WIFI frequencies refer to the different radio frequencies that WIFI devices use to communicate with each other. WIFI frequencies are divided into two frequency bands: the 2.4 GHz and 5 GHz bands. These bands are further divided into channels, each having its frequency.

The 2.4 GHz band is the most commonly used for WIFI connections since it is the only band supported by all WIFI devices. The 2.4 GHz band ranges from **2.400 GHz** to **2.4835 GHz**, and it is divided into 14 channels, each 5 MHz wide. However, the availability of channels may vary by region, and only channels 1 through 11 are commonly used in most countries.

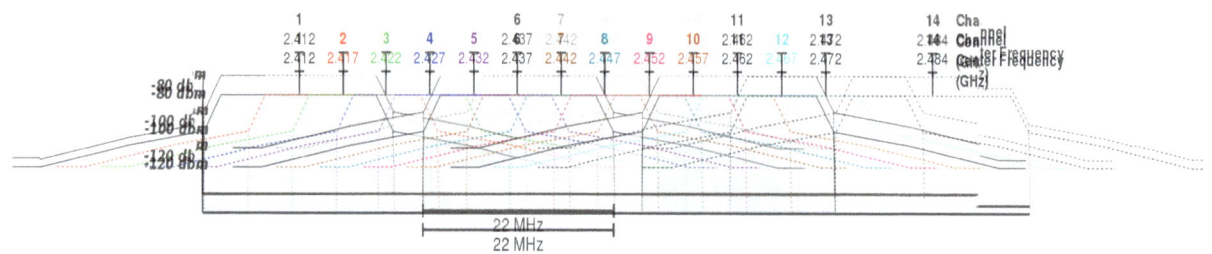

The 5 GHz band is less commonly used than the 2.4 GHz band since not all WIFI devices support it. This band consists of 23 channels, each spaced 20 MHz apart. The channels are 36-165, with channel 36 having the lowest frequency at **5.180 GHz** and channel 165 having the highest frequency at **5.825 GHz**. The use of different WIFI frequencies allows WIFI devices to communicate with each other without interference from other WIFI networks or other wireless devices. Using different channels enables WIFI networks to spread across a wide range of frequencies, reducing the chances of interference.

The WIFI 6 GHz band, extends WIFI's operational frequency range from **5.925 GHz** to **7.125 GHz**, offering a total of 1200 MHz of additional spectrum. This spectrum is divided into four sub-bands: U-NII-5 (5.925 GHz to 6.425 GHz); U-NII-6 (6.425 GHz to 6.525 GHz); U-NII-7 (6.525 GHz to 6.875 GHz); and U-NII-8 (6.875 GHz to 7.125 GHz). Within this band, WIFI networks can utilize up to 59 channels of 20 MHz each, along with wider 40 MHz, 80 MHz, and 160 MHz channels to accommodate faster speeds and lower latency.

EXPLAIN IT TO ME: WIFI

This added spectrum reduces congestion compared to the more crowded 2.4 GHz and 5 GHz bands, allowing for better performance in high-density environments. Additionally, technologies like Automated Frequency Coordination (AFC) ensure that unlicensed WIFI use in the 6 GHz band does not interfere with other licensed services that also occupy this space.

WIFI is also a technology based on the IEEE 802.11 standards, which define the physical and logical layers of the network. WIFI is a term that describes a wireless local area network (WLAN), which allows devices to connect to the Internet wirelessly. It is a way to connect to the Internet without using cables. The technology behind it is based on the IEEE 802.11 standards, which define the physical and logical layers of the network. WIFI has become a popular way to get connected to the Internet. It is widely available in public places such as airports, cafes, and hotels, as well as in homes and offices. It can be used to connect a variety of devices, including laptops, tablets, and smartphones. With WIFI, users can easily access the Internet, without the need for cables or any other additional hardware. This network is also very convenient since it allows users to move around without losing their connection.

WIFI has also been a popular choice for consumers for many years, as it provides a convenient and reliable way to access the internet in various settings. WIFI networks are becoming increasingly common, with most public places offering wireless access.

One of the primary benefits of having a good explanation of what WIFI is its convenience. WIFI allows users to access the internet from anywhere with a signal, allowing them to move around freely while still being connected. This has been especially useful for those who frequently travel, allowing them to stay connected while on the go. WIFI also allows users to access the internet without needing to install or configure any cables or hardware, making it easier to use than other forms of internet access. In addition to convenience,

WIFI also offers users a wide range of additional benefits. WIFI networks can provide users with faster internet speeds than traditional wired networks, making it ideal for applications such as streaming video or music, downloading large files, or playing online games. WIFI networks are also typically more secure than wired networks, making them a safer choice for online activities such as banking or shopping.

In conclusion, WIFI is a type of wireless network that allows devices to connect to the Internet or between other devices wirelessly. It is based on the IEEE 802.11 standards and is widely available in public places, homes, and offices. It is a convenient and easy way to connect to the Internet and allows users to move around without losing their connection.

EXPLAIN IT TO ME: WIFI

6. What is the difference between WIFI and LIFI?

WIFI and LIFI are two distinct wireless communications technologies, each with its characteristics and benefits. WIFI, short for Wireless Fidelity, operates in the radio frequency (RF) spectrum, typically using the 2.4 GHz, 5 GHz, or 6 GHz bands to transmit data wirelessly between devices. It has become the standard for wireless Internet connectivity in homes, businesses, and public spaces, providing reliable, high-speed data transmission over relatively long distances. WIFI signals can pass through walls and obstacles, allowing seamless communication between devices located in different rooms or areas of a building. This ubiquity and versatility have made WIFI an integral part of modern life, supporting a wide range of applications, from video streaming and web browsing to home automation and IoT (Internet of Things) devices. For more in-depth knowledge of LIFI, please reference the publication "**Explain It To Me: LIFI**".

In contrast, LIFI, sometimes written as Li-Fi or Light Fidelity, based on the IEEE 802.11bb standard, represents a relatively newer technology that uses visible or infrared light to transmit data wirelessly. Instead of radio waves, LIFI modulates the intensity of LED (light-emitting diode) bulbs to encode data, which is then received by light-sensitive receivers. This modulation process is invisible to the human eye, enabling high-speed data transmission while providing illumination. Unlike WIFI, LIFI signals are confined to the line of sight between the transmitter (LED bulb) and receiver because visible light cannot penetrate solid objects like walls or doors. This means that LIFI requires line of sight between devices for communication, making it more suitable for environments with line of sight and fewer obstacles.

EXPLAIN IT TO ME: WIFI

One of the main advantages of LIFI over WIFI is its ability to offer significantly higher data transmission speeds. Visible light has a much higher frequency than radio waves, which allows LIFI to support greater bandwidth and faster data rates. In the laboratory, LIFI has demonstrated speeds of up to several gigabits per second, far exceeding the capabilities of the fastest WIFI networks. This makes LIFI ideal for applications with critical high-speed data transmission, such as in dense urban environments, crowded public spaces, or scenarios requiring real-time communication and response.

Another advantage of LIFI is its immunity to electromagnetic interference (EMI), which can disrupt WIFI signals in crowded or cluttered RF environments. Since LIFI operates in the optical spectrum, RF interference from other electronic devices or wireless networks does not affect it, ensuring more reliable and consistent performance. Additionally, LIFI can be deployed in environments where RF communication is restricted or undesirable, such as hospitals, airplane cabins, and industrial facilities, without interfering with sensitive equipment or systems.

Despite these advantages, LIFI also has some limitations compared to WIFI. As mentioned earlier, LIFI signals require a direct line of sight between the transmitter and receiver, which limits its range and coverage compared to WIFI, which can transmit data over longer distances and through obstacles. Additionally, LIFI technology is still relatively new and may require specialized infrastructure and equipment for deployment, which could limit its widespread adoption and integration into existing wireless networks.

WIFI and LIFI represent two distinct approaches to wireless communication, each with its own strengths and limitations. WIFI offers ubiquity, flexibility, and longer range, making it well-suited for general-purpose wireless connectivity in various environments. On the other hand, LIFI provides the potential for higher data speeds, immunity to electromagnetic interference, and increased security, making it ideal for applications where high-speed, reliable wireless communication and security is essential. As both technologies evolve and mature, they will likely coexist and complement each other, providing users with a choice of wireless communications solutions tailored to their specific needs and requirements.

EXPLAIN IT TO ME: WIFI

7. What is the difference between WIFI and Bluetooth?

Bluetooth technology was invented by Dr. Jaap Haartsen, who is a Dutch electrical engineer, and his team at Ericsson, a telecommunications company, in the 1990s. They developed Bluetooth as a wireless communication technology to enable short-range data exchange between devices, such as mobile phones, computers, and peripherals, without the need for cables.

WIFI and Bluetooth, though both wireless communication technologies, cater to distinct needs and scenarios while also complementing each other seamlessly. WIFI, known for its robustness and widespread usage, operates on frequencies of 2.4 GHz, 5 GHz or 6 GHz, facilitating high-speed internet access and communication over larger distances, making it ideal for activities like streaming high-definition video, online gaming, and downloading hefty files.

In contrast, Bluetooth also operates within the 2.4 GHz frequency range and is designed for shorter-range communication, typically up to 30 feet. Its strengths lie in its efficiency and versatility, making it perfect for connecting peripherals such as headphones, speakers, keyboards, and mice to devices like computers and smartphones, as well as for transferring files between nearby devices.

The differences between WIFI and Bluetooth extend beyond range and frequency, encompassing factors like data transfer speed, power consumption, and susceptibility to interference. WIFI offers faster data transfer speeds but consumes more power, whereas Bluetooth is more energy-efficient, making it preferable for devices that prioritize battery life.

Additionally, WIFI is more susceptible to interference from other devices operating on the same frequency band or physical obstacles, whereas Bluetooth's shorter range helps mitigate potential conflicts. Despite their differences, WIFI and Bluetooth often work in tandem to provide users with comprehensive wireless connectivity solutions.

For instance, users can utilize WIFI for high-speed internet access and streaming while employing Bluetooth for connecting peripherals or transferring files locally between devices. This complementary relationship underscores the versatility and utility of both technologies in modern-day communication and networking.

EXPLAIN IT TO ME: WIFI

8. What are the benefits & cost savings of setting up a WIFI network?

Setting up your own network at work or home can be a great way to save on connection fees and maximize the benefits of a secure, reliable, and efficient network.

With a little time and effort, the cost savings and benefits of setting up your own network far outweigh the costs of relying on outside services.

First, setting up your own network will save you money on connection fees. In most cases, a single connection fee is needed to get your network up and running. This fee is typically much less than those associated with services requiring multiple connections and extra equipment.

The convenience and mobility that WIFI provides is an invaluable asset to those on the go. WIFI allows users to easily access the internet while they are away from home or work, allowing them to stay connected and productive.

One of the most significant benefits of WIFI in mobility is portability. WIFI-enabled devices can quickly be taken from place to place without worrying about plugging in a physical connection. This means that users can stay connected to the internet virtually wherever they are. Whether in a hotel room, a coffee shop, or an airport, users can stay connected to the internet without worrying about cords and cables. Another great advantage of WIFI is its increased speed compared to traditional connections.

WIFI connections are faster than wired connections, allowing users to access the internet quickly and easily. This means they can download large files, check emails, and stream videos without waiting long periods for their connection to be established. Another benefit of WIFI is connecting multiple devices to one network. WIFI allows users to connect various devices to the same network, allowing them to share a single connection. This means that users can access the internet from multiple devices without using multiple connections. This is especially useful for those who need to access the internet from multiple devices, such as laptops and phones.

Additionally, setting up your own network will allow you to avoid extra fees associated with rental equipment, additional services, and installation fees. Second, setting up your own network offers many benefits in terms of reliability and efficiency.

By controlling your network, you can ensure that your network is secure and reliable. This can be especially beneficial for businesses that need to secure and confidential sensitive data. Additionally, setting up your network will allow you to customize your network to meet the needs of your business or home. This can help you maximize efficiency and ensure your network is as efficient as possible.

EXPLAIN IT TO ME: WIFI

Finally, setting up your network can offer peace of mind. With a secure network, you can rest assured that your data is safe and secure. Additionally, you can ensure your network is not vulnerable to outside attacks or malicious software.

This can help you avoid costly repairs and data losses that outside sources can cause. Overall, setting up your own network can be a great way to save money on connection fees and maximize the benefits of a secure, reliable, and efficient network.

By controlling your network, you can save money and ensure that your network is secure and efficient. Additionally, knowing that your data is secure and your network is not vulnerable to outside attacks, you can have peace of mind.

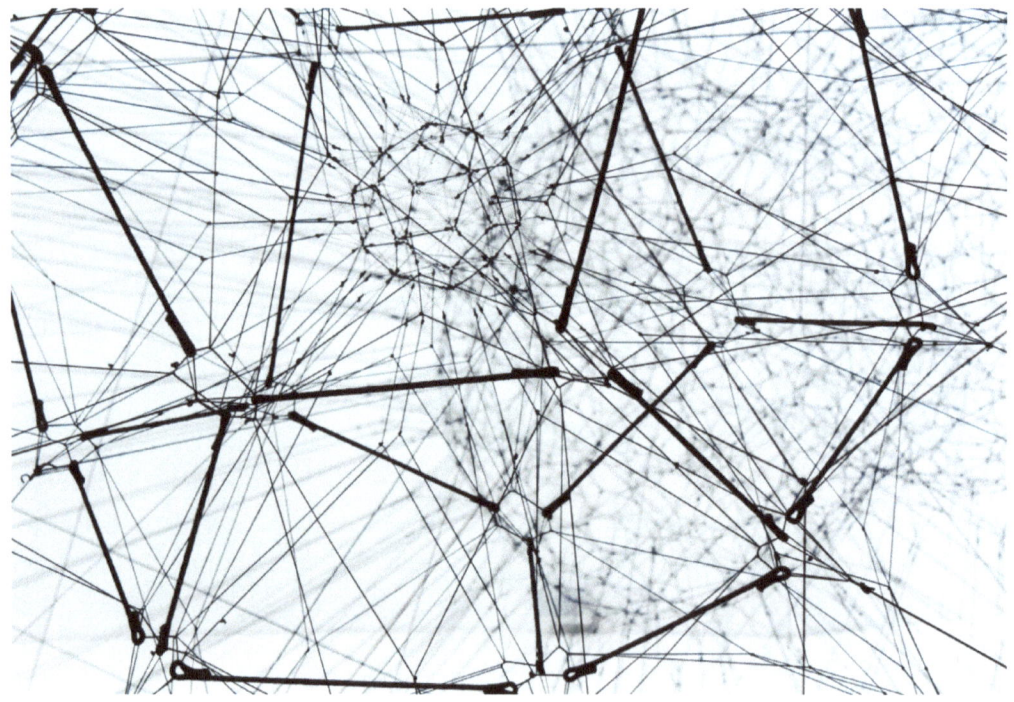

EXPLAIN IT TO ME: WIFI

9. What do I need to know before setting up a WIFI network?

Setting up WIFI can seem intimidating, but it is quite a simple process. The benefits of having WIFI are vast and can help you stay connected with the rest of the world. The first step to setting up WIFI is to purchase a router.

The router acts as the central hub for your home network. Once the router is plugged in, it can connect to either a modem or a cable outlet (*note: some ISP modems can also act as routers*). The router will then create a wireless network for all of your devices to connect to. Once the router is connected, the next step is configuring the settings. This includes setting up a secure password for your network, setting up a network name, and setting up encryption. The password should be secure and not easily guessed, and the encryption should be set to WPA2 or higher. Once the settings are configured, the WIFI connection can be tested.

The router should be able to detect the devices that are connected and should be able to provide internet access to them. The WIFI network should be up and running if everything is working correctly. The benefits of having WIFI are numerous. It allows you to stay connected with the rest of the world, and it can save you the hassle of using cables for all your devices. It also allows for more flexibility and convenience when accessing the internet.

Setting up WIFI can be a bit of a hassle, but the benefits are worth the effort. Once set up, you can enjoy the convenience of connecting to the internet from anywhere in your home. With WIFI, you can stay connected with the rest of the world and make the most out of your internet connection.

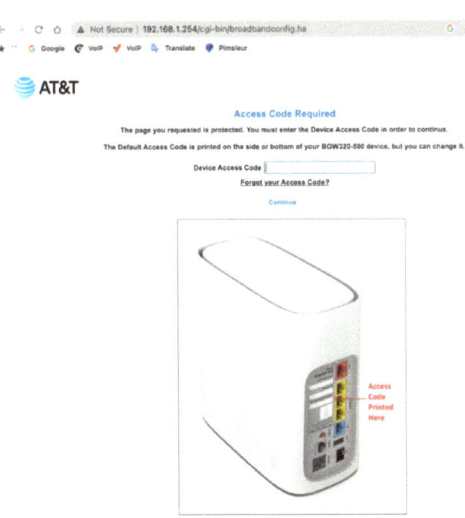

EXPLAIN IT TO ME: WIFI

10. What top technologies do I need to consider for a WIFI network?

The top twelve technologies used by Internet Service Providers (ISP) are as follows:

1. DSL (Digital Subscriber Line) DSL is a popular technology used to connect Internet modems to their network. It is an always-on connection that uses existing telephone lines to connect to the Internet. Depending on the package, DSL speeds can range from 256 Kbps to over 40 Mbps.

2. Cable Modem Cable modems are used to connect Internet modems to their network by using the same coaxial cable that carries television signals. Cable modems typically offer speeds ranging from 10 Mbps to 100 Mbps.

3. Fiber Optic Fiber optic technology is used to connect Internet modems to their network. Fiber optic cables are thin strands of glass that can transmit large amounts of data at high speeds. Fiber optic connections can range from 10 Mbps to 1 Gbps.

4. Satellite technology is used to connect Internet modems to their network by using a satellite dish. This connection is often used in rural areas where other forms of broadband are unavailable. Satellite connections are usually slower than other forms of broadband and can range from 512 Kbps to 10 Mbps.

5. Wireless technology is used to connect Internet modems to their network using radio frequencies. Wireless connections usually offer speeds of up to 54 Mbps and can be used to connect multiple computers to the Internet.

6. Mobile Broadband Mobile broadband is used to connect Internet modems to their network by using cellular networks. Mobile broadband speeds can range from 3G (3rd Generation) to 5G (5th Generation). 3G speeds range from 384 Kbps to 3 Mbps, while 5G speeds range from 20 Mbps to 100+ Mbps.

7. Dial-up is an older technology used to connect Internet modems to their network using a regular telephone line. Dial-up connections are the slowest type of connection available, and speeds range from 56 Kbps to 256 Kbps.

8. ISDN (Integrated Services Digital Network) is a digital phone service used to connect Internet modems to their network. ISDN speeds can range from 64 Kbps to 128 Kbps, depending on the package.

EXPLAIN IT TO ME: WIFI

9: WiMax is a wireless technology used to connect Internet modems to their network using radio frequencies. WiMax speeds can range from 3 Mbps to 10 Mbps depending on the package.

10: Powerline technology which is used to connect Internet modems to their network by using existing electrical wiring. Depending on the package, powerline speeds can range from 10 Mbps to 200 Mbps.

11: Ethernet is a wired technology used to connect Internet modems to their network. Ethernet cables are typically used to connect computers to modems, and speeds can range from 10 Mbps to 1 Gbps depending on the package.

12: Broadband over Power Lines (BPL) is a technology used to connect Internet modems to their network using existing electrical wiring. Depending on the package, BPL speeds can range from 1 Mbps to 10 Mbps.

EXPLAIN IT TO ME: WIFI

11. How does Speed & Latency impact WIFI?

Speed and latency are two of the most critical factors in determining the performance of a gaming system. They both play a significant role in the overall gaming experience. WIFI speed is the measure of how quickly the game can process input from the player. The higher the speed, the smoother and more responsive the gameplay will be. The game can become unresponsive or laggy when the speed is too low. This can lead to frustration and a decrease in overall performance.

Internet modems come with various speed ranges, all of which are measured in Kbps (Kilobits per second), Mbps (Megabits per second), and Gbps (Gigabits per second). Simply put, these terms refer to the amount of data that can be sent or received in a given amount of time.

Kbps stands for Kilobits per second and is the smallest data transfer rate measurement. It is generally used to measure slow speeds, such as those of older modems, ranging from 56Kbps to dial-up speeds of up to around 200Kbps. Kbps are also used to measure the speed of specific mobile broadband networks and satellite connections.

Mbps stands for Megabits per second and is the most commonly used measure for internet speeds. It measures the speed of most modern modems, which typically range from 1Mbps to 100Mbps. This is enough to handle most online activities, such as streaming and downloading movies.

Gbps stands for Gigabits per second and is the highest measure of data transfer rate. It is generally used to measure the speed of fiber-optic connections, ranging from 100Mbps to 1Gbps. This is enough to handle multiple online activities at once easily and is more than enough for gaming and HD video streaming activities. In summary, Kbps measures slow speeds, Mbps measures the speed of most modern modems, and Gbps measures the speed of fiber-optic connections. The speeds range from 56Kbps to 1Gbps, depending on the type of modem and connection.

Latency measures how long it takes for an action to be processed and displayed on the screen. Low latency will result in a more immersive and realistic gaming experience. High latency can cause delays in the game, making it feel unresponsive and slow.

Both WIFI speed and latency are essential when it comes to achieving maximum performance in a gaming system. When combined, they create a smooth, responsive, and enjoyable gaming experience.

EXPLAIN IT TO ME: WIFI

WIFI speed and latency should be monitored and adjusted to ensure the best performance possible. Overall, the importance of Wii speed and latency for performance cannot be overstated.

A gaming system that is not optimized for these two factors will result in a poor gaming experience. By monitoring and adjusting these two factors, gamers can ensure that their gaming system runs at its highest potential.

EXPLAIN IT TO ME: WIFI

12. How does Security impact WIFI?

With the ever-increasing number of connected devices, the way we protect our data is becoming more critical than ever, and as such, understanding the different types of WIFI security is essential for keeping our data safe. At its core, WIFI security is based on encryption.

Encryption is a process where data is converted into a meaningless format and decrypted back into its original form. It's used to protect data from unauthorized access. The most commonly used WIFI security protocols are **WPA** (WIFI Protected Access), **WPA2** (WIFI Protected Access 2), and **WPA3** (WIFI Protected Access 3).

WPA was the first version of the WIFI security protocol to be widely adopted, and it is still the most used today. It is based on the TKIP (Temporal Key Integrity Protocol) encryption protocol and provides good security. WPA2 was released as a more secure version and is based on the AES (Advanced Encryption Standard) encryption protocol.

WPA2 is much stronger than WPA and is the most secure option available today. In addition to WPA and WPA2, several other security protocols are available. WEP (Wired Equivalent Privacy) is an older protocol that is rarely used today due to its lack of security.

WPA3, requires an attacker to interact with your WIFI for every password guess that they have to make, making it much harder and time-consuming to crack.

WPS (WIFI Protected Setup) is a protocol designed to make it easier for users to set up their networks. It is not as secure as WPA and WPA2, but it is still helpful in setting up networks quickly. Another critical aspect of WIFI security is the use of passwords. A strong password is essential for keeping your network secure. It should be at least eight characters in length and contain a mixture of both upper and lowercase letters, numbers, and symbols. It is also a good idea to change your password regularly to ensure your data remains secure.

Finally, it is also essential to be aware of the security features available on your router. Many routers have firewalls and wireless isolation features that can make your network more secure. It is vital to make sure that these features are enabled and that your router is kept up to date with the very latest security updates and patches. In conclusion, it is very beneficial to understand the different types of WIFI security protocols and how you can use them to keep your data safe.

By using the most secure protocols, such as WPA2 or WPA3 and strong passwords, you can ensure that your data is kept safe from unauthorized access.

EXPLAIN IT TO ME: WIFI

13. How do I set up a WIFI network?

Establishing a wireless network at home or in the workplace can be intimidating. However, with a bit of knowledge and preparation, it can be done relatively quickly.

The first step in setting up a wireless network is to determine the type of equipment needed. This will depend on the size of the network, the number of users, and the range of coverage. Wireless routers, adapters, and access points are the most common hardware used in a wireless network.

The router will provide the connection to the internet, the adapter will allow for a wired connection, and the access point will provide the wireless connection.

Next, the network should be configured. This will involve setting up the SSID (Service Set Identifier) and encryption key, providing security for the connection. It is also essential to choose the correct frequency band, as this will determine the range of the network. After this step, make sure that the router is properly connected. This will involve connecting the router to the internet and any other devices that need to access the network.

If there are multiple devices, it is essential to make sure that the router is configured correctly to allow for multiple connections. Once the network is up and running, it is important to ensure that the security settings are correctly configured. This includes setting up firewalls, as well as making sure that the encryption key is secure.

It is also important to ensure that the router's firmware is up to date to protect against vulnerabilities. Finally, it is essential to monitor the network regularly. This will ensure that the network runs optimally and that any potential issues can be addressed quickly. When setting up a wireless network, it is crucial to consider the size of the network, the number of users, the range of coverage, and the security settings.

Taking the time to configure the network properly will ensure the connection is secure and reliable. With the proper preparation and knowledge, setting up a wireless network at home or in the workplace can be a straightforward and rewarding process.

EXPLAIN IT TO ME: WIFI

14. What is the Internet modem & what does it have to do with WIFI?

An Internet modem is a hardware device used for connection of a computer or other device to the internet. It is typically provided by an Internet Service Provider (ISP). The modem acts as a connection bridge between the local area network (LAN) and the internet.

It receives data signals from the ISP, converts them into a form that can be used by the computer, and sends out any data that the computer needs to send to the ISP. The modem is the actual hardware device that is connected to the computer. A modem can consist of a router component and a modem component. In this scenario, this hybrid device will connect to the ISP and allow the computer to access the internet. This hybrid device receives the data signals from the ISP and converts them into a form that the computer can use. The device then sends the data to one of its output ports, which then sends the data to the computer that is connected to that port. The modem-router also performs other functions, such as providing a secure connection to the ISP, allowing for WIFI access to the internet, providing network security, and providing other network services such as **DNS** and **DHCP**.

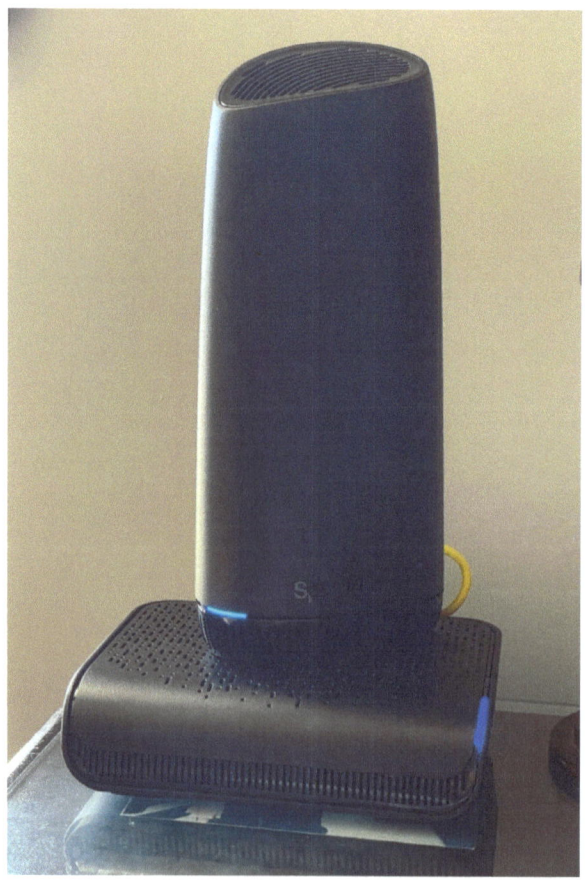

EXPLAIN IT TO ME: WIFI

An Internet modem (or modem-router hybrid device) is essential for connecting a computer or other device to the internet. It is typically provided by an ISP and is usually included in the cost of the internet service. The modem router provides the secure connection to the ISP, and the modem provides the actual link to the computer or other device. Together, they allow for a fast and reliable connection to the internet.

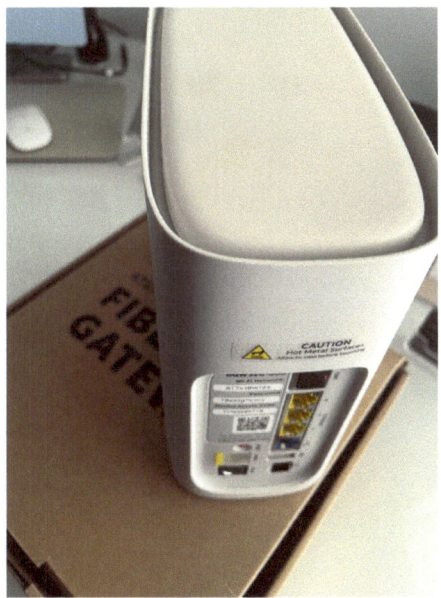

EXPLAIN IT TO ME: WIFI

15. What is the Router & what does it have to do with WIFI?

A wireless router is a device that allows connection to the internet via a modem and allows multiple devices to access the internet at the same time. It is the main component of a wireless home network and acts as a gateway between the internet and all the connected devices.

Wireless routers typically contain a built-in **firewall** to protect the network from malicious attacks and viruses. They also come with various features, such as parental controls, guest networks, and media streaming capabilities.

Wireless routers are easy to set up, and most come with step-by-step instructions to get you up and running. In many instances a router is not necessary, because most Internet modems have a two or four port built in router component. In the scenario, where your device is a modem only (and is not a modem-router hybrid device), you will need to connect the router to your modem and a power source, then configure the router using the software provided. Once set up, you can connect devices such as laptops, tablets, and smartphones to the network via WIFI.

Additionally, many wireless routers come with an Ethernet port, which allows you to connect wired devices such as desktop computers and gaming consoles. Wireless routers come in various sizes and speeds to meet different needs. The router's speed is determined by the number of antennas and the frequency at which it operates. The higher the speed, the more devices it can support and the faster it can stream media. Additionally, the router's range is determined by the number and type of antennas it has.

Newer, dual-band routers can operate on both the 2.4 GHz, 5 GHz, and 6 GHz frequencies, offering higher speeds and a wider range than single-band routers. Overall, a wireless router is useful for connecting multiple devices to the internet and creating a home network. With the right router, you can enjoy fast and reliable internet access, as well as access to a variety of features.

But you might ask the question, how do I go about selecting a wireless router?

> When selecting a router, the first step is to identify the purpose of the router. Wireless routers provide wireless access to the internet or other networked devices. This means that the router must be compatible with the user's internet connection. For example, if the user has a cable internet connection, they must purchase a router that is compatible with that connection.

EXPLAIN IT TO ME: WIFI

The next step is to determine the network speed the user needs. This is important because it will determine the type of router the user needs. Since different routers offer different speeds, so it's important to select a router that can handle the amount of data you will be transferring over the network.

The third step is to determine the range of the router. This will depend on the size of the space the user wants to cover. If the user has a large area, they will need to purchase a router with a more extended range.

Finally, the user should consider any walls or other obstructions that may affect the router's range. Finally, the user should consider the cost of the router. They should compare the different routers on the market and decide which one best fits their needs. Additionally, the user should consider the cost of any additional equipment that may be needed, such as antennas or additional ports.

Some routers offer additional security features, such as a firewall, to protect your network from malicious attacks. It's crucial to select a router that provides the highest level of security. Finally, you need to consider your budget when choosing a router. While some routers may offer the latest features and the highest speeds, they may also be more expensive. Finding a router that fits your budget while still offering the features and rates you need is essential. Selecting the right router is an important decision.

Remember, the router you select is critical in setting up a home network. It is essential to select the correct router because it can affect your network's speed, reliability, and security. When selecting a router, there are several factors to consider. The first is the type of router.

Once you have a router, you will need to connect it to your network to access the internet. This process can be a bit intimidating at first; however, with the proper steps, it can be completed quickly and easily. The first step is to plug the router into a power outlet.

Once it is powered on, you must connect a network cable from your modem to the router. This is typically done through the WAN port on the router. Make sure the line is firmly connected at both ends. Now, you will need to access the router's settings to configure it. To do this, open your internet browser and type in the router's IP address. This can usually be found on the bottom of the router or in the manual.

Once you have gained access to the router settings, you will need to configure the settings accordingly. You will need to configure the router's IP address, subnet mask, gateway, and DNS. The IP address should not be already being used on the network, and the gateway should be the same as the one used by your modem. The subnet mask should be 255.255.255.0, and your internet service provider should provide the DNS.

EXPLAIN IT TO ME: WIFI

Once you have configured the settings, you need to save them and restart the router. You can do this by going to the router's settings page and clicking on the "Restart" button. After the router has restarted, you can test the connection by opening your internet browser and visiting a website. Now that the router is connected to the network, you will need to configure the wireless settings. To do this, you will need to access the router's settings page once again. Here, you will need to configure the SSID (wireless network name), the security type, and the password.

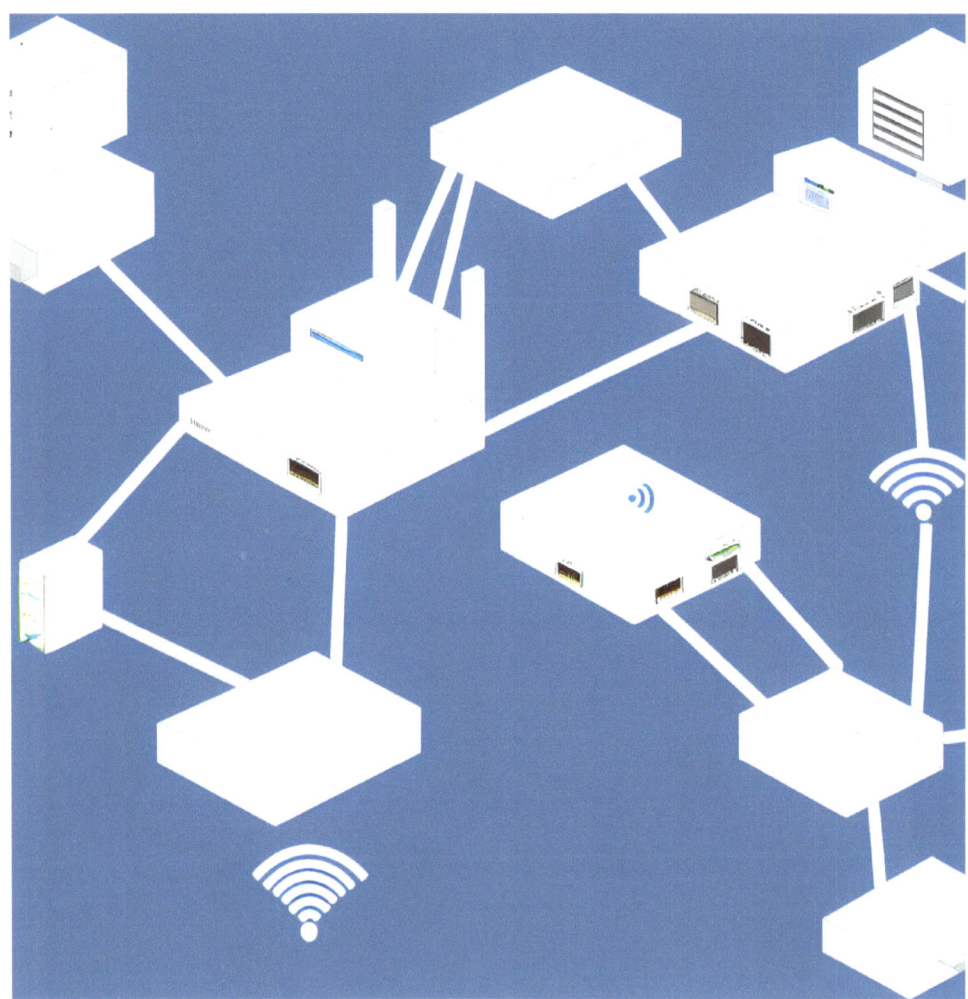

Setting a network name or unique **SSID** (Service Set Identifier) used to identify a particular wireless network is essential. The SSID is an alphanumeric string containing of up to 32 characters. It is made up of a combination of letters, numbers, and even special characters, depending on the wireless router being used.

EXPLAIN IT TO ME: WIFI

A wireless network typically consists of one or more access points that are connected to a wired network and provide wireless access to all the devices within range of the access points. The wireless access points broadcast the SSID to allow devices to connect to the wireless network. When a device scans for available networks, the SSID is displayed in the list of wireless networks that the device can connect to. When devices attempt to connect to a wireless network, they must select the correct SSID in order to establish a connection.

This is why it is essential to know the SSID of the wireless network you wish to connect to. If the wrong SSID is selected, the devices will not be able to connect to the network. The SSID is also used to control access to the wireless network.

The SSID can create different levels of access, such as allowing only specific users to access the network or blocking certain devices from connecting to the network. The SSID can also encrypt the sent and received data on the wireless network.

Setting a specific network name is essential also for a variety of reasons. It allows you to quickly identify your network among the many other wireless networks in your area and distinguish it from other networks that use the identical SSID.

Additionally, it allows you to control access to your network by setting a password and restricting users who do not have the necessary credentials. When configuring your network, you have the option to broadcast the SSID or keep it hidden. Broadcasting your SSID can make your network easier to find and connect to, but it also allows others to discover your network and possibly gain unauthorized access. On the other hand, keeping your SSID hidden can make it more difficult for others to find and connect to your network, but it also makes it harder for legitimate users to access the network.

It is recommended to broadcast your SSID, but you should also set a strong password for additional security. Another important aspect of setting a specific network name is that it can help protect your network from interference from other wireless networks in your area that use the identical SSID.

This is because your router will recognize the network name and will be able to differentiate it from other networks. If two networks use the same SSID, it can cause interference and make it difficult for users to connect to the correct network. Overall, setting a specific network name, along with a strong password, is an essential step in ensuring the security of your network. It gives you control over who has access to your network and helps protect it from interference from other wireless networks. Additionally, broadcasting your SSID makes it easier for legitimate users to connect to your network while keeping it hidden can help protect it from unauthorized access.

EXPLAIN IT TO ME: WIFI

As a standard practice, it may be wise to set an additional guest SSID with its own unique password. This allows for an additional network that can be configured in your router that has limited functionality that an occasional visitor can use. The limits often allow only for pass-through connection to the internet and will not allow a visitor that connects to your WIFI network to update the main configuration.

You will also want to ensure the security type and password are vital, as this will help protect your network from hackers. For a wired connection, you'll need to connect the router to the modem, then configure the settings as required by your ISP. You'll need to connect the router to the modem for a wireless connection, then configure the settings as directed by your ISP and set up the wireless network.

You'll also need to test the new router to ensure it is working correctly. This includes testing the connection speed, checking the security settings, and ensuring all features function correctly. If the tests are successful, you can begin using the router and enjoy the added features and improved performance.

Once you have configured the wireless settings, you need to save them and restart the router. After the router has restarted, you can test the connection by connecting a laptop or mobile device to the network. If the relationship is successful, you have successfully connected your router to the network.

Again, the right router can ensure that your home network runs smoothly and securely. It's essential to take the time to research and compare routers to make sure you select the one that is best suited for your needs.

EXPLAIN IT TO ME: WIFI

16. What is a Firewall or VPN & what does it have to do with WIFI?

A **firewall** is a network security system used to monitor, verify and control all incoming and outgoing network traffic based on pre-configured security rules. It acts as a barrier between a trusted internal network and an untrusted external network (i.e., the Internet).

Firewalls can be hardware-based, software-based, or a combination of both. A hardware firewall is typically a dedicated device placed between the internal and external networks. It generally is a rack-mountable appliance that contains network interface cards and specialized software.

A software firewall can exist as a program installed on a computer and designed to filter network traffic. The primary objective of a firewall is to block unauthorized access to a private network while allowing authorized communications. It can also monitor and log network activity, detect and prevent malicious activity, and block certain types of traffic.

Firewalls can be configured to allow certain types of traffic, such as web traffic, while blocking others, such as peer-to-peer applications. Firewalls can also limit access to certain websites, applications, and services. Firewalls are essential to any network security system and can provide a first line of defense against malicious attacks.

A **VPN**, or **Virtual Private Network**, is usually a software security measure that is used to protect a user's data while they are connected to a public or unsecured WIFI network. A VPN (i.e., Nord, ShurfShark, TunnelBear, or Express) encrypts the user's connection, providing an extra layer of security and privacy. This helps to ensure that hackers, identity thieves, and other malicious actors are not able to intercept the user's data.

When users connect to a public WIFI network, their data is sent over an unsecured connection. This means that anyone accessing the same network can intercept the data and potentially access sensitive information. To combat this, a VPN program can be started to create a secure, encrypted tunnel between the user's device and the WIFI network. This tunnel can originate in the user's home city and terminate in another major city or country. Essentially, when used, you have put your device in another geographical location. It ensures that any data sent over the network (from a public place or store) is encrypted and protected from potential attackers.

It is vital to ensure firewalls and VPNs are correctly configured and maintained to provide the necessary protection.

EXPLAIN IT TO ME: WIFI

17.   What is a Switch & what does it have to do with WIFI?

A switch is an optional product that allows users to connect to the internet. It is a piece of networking hardware that enables users to link multiple devices together in a network. It is often used in homes, offices, and organizations to create a local area network (LAN).

A switch allows a user to connect multiple devices to the same router. This is done by connecting the switch to the router via an Ethernet cable. Once the switch is connected, the user can connect multiple devices using additional Ethernet cables. All of these devices will be able to access the router and the internet.

Switches can also connect multiple routers, allowing for a more extensive and more complex network. This is often referred to as a vast area network (WAN). By connecting multiple routers together; users can access the internet from multiple locations and share resources with other users on the network.

Switches have many other uses in addition to allowing users to connect to the internet. They can be used to prioritize network traffic or to create virtual Local Area Networks (VLANs). They can also be used to increase the security of a network by providing extra layers of authentication and encryption.

In summary, a switch is an optional product that allows a user to connect multiple devices to the same router or multiple routers to create a large and complex network. It provides a secure and reliable connection to the internet and can be used to prioritize network traffic or to create virtual Local Area Networks (VLANs).

EXPLAIN IT TO ME: WIFI

18.   What is an Access Point & what does it have to do with WIFI?

An **Access Point** (AP) is a device that allows wireless devices to connect to a wired network. It usually consists of a wireless router, an access point, and a network switch. Sometimes an access point is referred to as a **Hotspot.**

The AP connects the wireless device (cell phone, laptop, smartphone, tablet, etc.) and the wired network (such as a home or corporate network). Many AP devices use **Power over Ethernet** (or **PoE)** as opposed to a separate power supply. The access point acts as a bridge between wireless devices and the wired network. It receives the wireless signal from the wireless device and converts it into a signal that the wired network can understand.

The access point also transmits data from the wired network to the wireless devices. Many access points are mounted on the ceiling due to their strategic positioning. This allows for maximum coverage of the wireless signal throughout the building and helps avoid interference with other wireless devices. Having the access point mounted on the ceiling also allows for easy access to the access point for maintenance. This type of installation is highly recommended.

if needed. Additionally, mounting the access point on the ceiling allows it to be out of the way of people and other obstacles, which can reduce interference with the wireless signal.

Overall, an internet access point is an important device that allows wireless devices to conveniently and safely connect to a wired network. Mounting the access point on the ceiling can provide maximum coverage, avoid interference, and allow for easy access for maintenance.

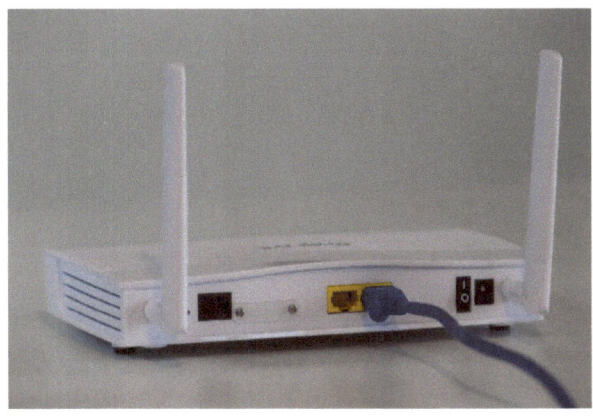

EXPLAIN IT TO ME: WIFI

19. What do NIC cards have to do with WIFI?

The short answer is nothing. A network interface card (NIC) is a hardware device or internal computer component that allows a direct physical connection to a local area network (LAN).

The NIC is the physical link between a computer and a network. It is responsible for transmitting and receiving data between the two. It typically consists of a printed circuit board with several connectors, transceivers, and other components. It is an essential component of any computer network and enables computers to communicate with each other. The NIC typically has several connectors, including one or more RJ-45 ports for connecting to an Ethernet network, an RJ-11 port for connecting to a telephone line, and a USB port for connecting external devices.

The NIC also includes transceivers, which are responsible for transmitting and receiving data. To use it, the user must first install the appropriate drivers. The user can then configure the NIC's settings, such as the IP address, network mask, gateway address, and other parameters usually stored in a configuration file on the computer. The NIC is responsible for authentication and security (so that only an authorized user is allowed access to the network). It is also responsible for encrypting data before it is sent across the network and ensuring that only authorized users can access the data.

EXPLAIN IT TO ME: WIFI

20. What do Streaming devices have to do with WIFI?

A streaming device uses WIFI to access content from various internet streaming services. These devices connect to a wireless network and allow users to stream their favorite movies, TV shows, and music.

Roku, Apple, Chromecast, TiVo, and other streaming devices come with a variety of features, such as the ability to access over 400,000 movies and TV episodes, access to thousands of music channels, access to more than 1,000 apps and games, and access to more than 350,000 free and paid channels.

Roku and Apple devices also offer voice control, so you can search for content using your voice, as well as a remote control that makes it easy to navigate the streaming content.

Apple devices, such as the Apple TV, also use WIFI to access streaming content. They offer access to Apple TV+ and Apple Music, as well as access to the iTunes store and the App Store. They also come with a variety of features, such as the ability to stream content to multiple devices, use AirPlay to stream content from your iOS device, and access content from other streaming services such as Netflix and Hulu. With streaming devices such as Roku and Apple devices, you can easily and quickly access your favorite content from the comfort of your own home or car (i.e., CarPlay).

All you need is a WIFI connection, and you can start streaming.

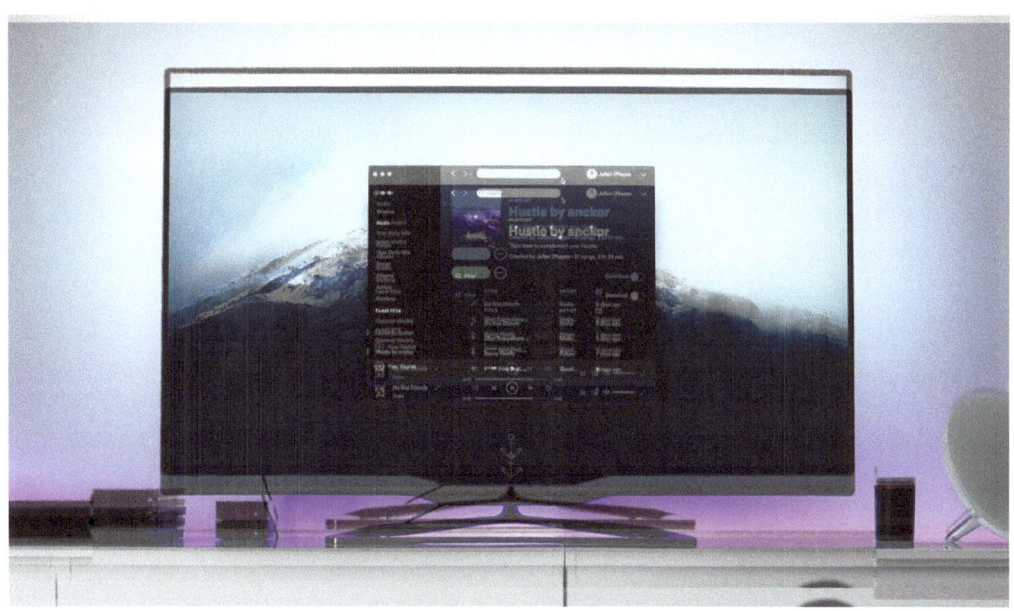

EXPLAIN IT TO ME: WIFI

21. How do I connect devices to the WIFI network?

Before beginning the process of connecting devices to a network, it is essential to consider the different types of networks and the standards they use. For example, the 802.11b standard is used for wired networks, while "802.11n – bn" is the standard for wireless networks. WIFI 3, 4, 5, 6, 7 and 8 are and will be the standards for newer wireless networks.

Generation	IEEE Standard	Accepted	Max link rate	Radio Frequency (GHz)
Wi-Fi 8	802.11 bn	2028?	100,000	2.4, 5, 6
Wi-Fi 7	802.11 be	2024	0.4 - 23,059	2.4, 5, 6
Wi-Fi 6E	802.11 ax	2021	0.4 - 9608	2.4, 5, 6
Wi-Fi 6	802.11 ax	2021	0.4 - 9608	2.4, 5
Wi-Fi 5	802.11 ac	2013	6.5 - 6933	5
Wi-Fi 4	802.11 n	2009	6.5 - 600	2.4, 5
Wi-Fi 3	802.11 g	2003	6 - 54	2.4
Wi-Fi 2	802.11 a	1999	6 - 54	5
Wi-Fi 1	802.11 b	1999	1-11	2.4
Wi-Fi 0	802.11	1997	1-2	2.4

Once the type of network is determined, the next step is to choose the best method for connecting the devices to the network. A physical connection is necessary for wired networks, typically via an Ethernet cable. For wireless networks, the devices must have a wireless radio, such as a WIFI card, to connect to the network.

Once the device has the necessary hardware, the next step is to configure the device to connect to the network. For wired networks, this typically involves setting up an IP address, network mask, and gateway and configuring other settings, such as DNS servers.

For wireless networks, the settings will vary depending on the type of security being used, such as WEP, WPA, WPA2 or WPA3. Once the settings are configured, the device can be connected to the network. For wired networks, this is usually done by plugging the Ethernet cable into the device and the network port. The device must detect the network for wireless networks, which can be done by searching for available networks.

EXPLAIN IT TO ME: WIFI

Once the network is detected, the device can be connected by entering the security information if necessary. Once the device is connected, the user can access the network resources. Depending on the type of network, the user may need to enter authentication information, such as a username and password, to access the network.

Connecting devices to a network can be a straightforward process. Still, there are several factors to consider, such as the type of network and the appropriate standards to use, the best method for connecting the device, and the necessary settings. Following these steps allows devices to be quickly and easily connected to a network.

EXPLAIN IT TO ME: WIFI

22. How do I make a software connection to a WIFI network?

Using software to connect to a wireless network is a relatively simple task.

The first step is to either connect to or open the wireless network software on your device (i.e., computer, cell phone, media player, TV). This will usually be located in the taskbar's system tray or notification area. Once opened, a list of wireless networks should be presented.

Look for the name of the wireless network you wish to connect to. Once located, select it and then click the "connect" button. Depending on the type of network, you may be prompted to enter a password or passphrase. You can skip this step if the web is open and doesn't require a password.

Once the password has been entered, click the "connect" button again. The software should then attempt to connect to the wireless network. If the connection is successful, you will usually see a notification in the system tray or notification area. If the connection is not successful, you may need to verify the wireless network settings.

Make sure that the encryption type matches the type set on the software. If the encryption type is incorrect, then the connection will fail. Once the connection has been established, you can access the internet or other services.

Depending on the type of wireless network, you may need to enter a username and password to gain access. If the wireless network connection is not working as expected, you can try restarting the software or rebooting the device. This should reset the connection and allow for a successful connection to the wireless network.

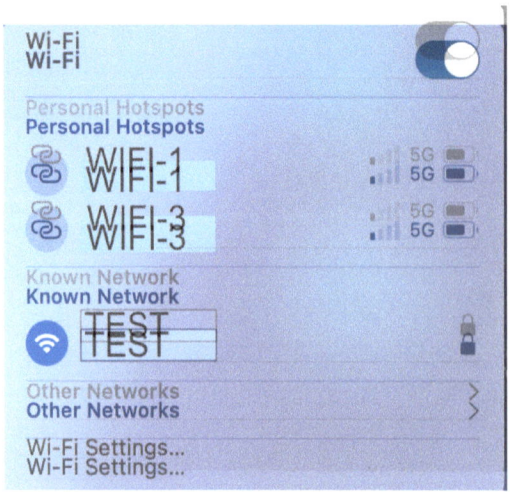

EXPLAIN IT TO ME: WIFI

23. How do I troubleshoot problems with a WIFI network?

Troubleshooting a wireless network can take time and effort. Fortunately, there are several popular tools available to help. These tools can help identify common problems such as interference, signal strength, speed, and range, as well as more complex issues related to authentication, encryption, and security.

A wireless analyzer is one of the most popular tools for troubleshooting wireless networks. A wireless analyzer is a software application that scans the airwaves and collects data about the available networks. It can detect various information, such as signal strength, channel usage, and network performance. This data can then be used to identify potential problems and suggest solutions.

Speed test tools are used to troubleshoot wireless networks by providing users with information about their wireless network performance. Speed test tools measure the network's download and upload speeds, latency, and jitter. They also provide detailed information about the network's performance and the amount of data transmitted or received.

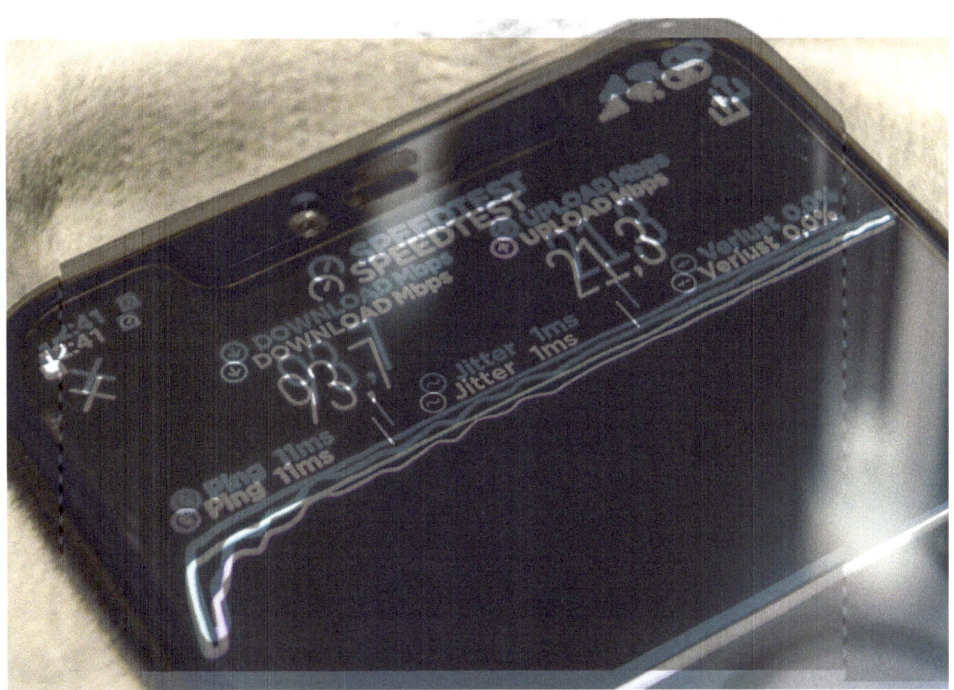

EXPLAIN IT TO ME: WIFI

Another popular tool is a wireless sniffer. A wireless sniffer is a software application that monitors the traffic on a wireless network. It can detect unauthorized access, identify data leakage, and monitor performance. It can also be used to detect rogue access points, which are access points that are not authorized to be on the network.

Here is a guide on basic troubleshooting steps that can be done to determine problems for a wireless network:

Step 1: Check the Wireless Router The first step in troubleshooting a wireless network is ensuring the router is functioning correctly. Sometimes rebooting the device may help. Check the router's connection and ensure that all cables are properly connected. Also, check the power light on the router and ensure it is lit up.

Step 2: Check the Wireless Signal The next step is to check the wireless signal. You can use a wireless signal strength meter or a laptop with a wireless card. The strength should be at least 50%. If it is lower than that, you may need to move the router to another location to get a better signal.

Step 3: Check the Wireless Card. If the wireless signal is strong, the next step is to check the wireless card. Ensure it is enabled and the drivers are up to date. You can use Windows Device Manager to check the status of the device.

Step 4: Check the Network Settings. If the wireless card is working correctly, the next step is to check the network settings. Ensure the wireless network is set to the correct channel, encryption type, and SSID. If the settings are incorrect, you may need to reset the router or change the settings manually.

Step 5: Check the Network Adapter The last step is to check the network adapter. Ensure it is enabled and the drivers are up to date. Again, you can use Windows Device Manager to prevent the device's status.

Once you have completed all of these steps, you should be able to troubleshoot your wireless network. If the problem persists, you may need to contact your ISP for further assistance.

EXPLAIN IT TO ME: WIFI

24. Definitions

802.11 - a family of wireless networking standards important for local area networking. It is the basis of most wireless networks today and allows devices to communicate with each other without the need for wires. 802.11 is important because it enables users to access the internet and connect to other devices over a wireless network, making it much easier to stay connected. The 802.11 protocol family includes 802.11a, 802.11b, 802.11g, 802.11n, 802.11ac, 802.11ax, and 802.11be. These protocols are designed to provide high-speed network communication with low latency, using either the 2.4 GHz, 5 GHz, or 6 GHz frequencies. Each protocol offers different features, including data rates, range, and security features.

Access Point - An access point is a wireless device that bridges a wired network and wireless-enabled devices. It can be mounted in various places, such as walls, ceilings, or even on desks. Access points allow wireless devices to access the internet or a network and can be used for a range of applications, such as streaming media and file sharing,

DHCP (or **Dynamic Host Configuration Protocol**) is a network protocol used to assign new IP addresses to networked devices dynamically. It is an essential tool for networks because it helps ensure that each device on the web has a unique IP address and can quickly and easily connect to the network (i.e., by assigning a network address -192.168.x.x).

DNS (or Domain Name System, i.e., "**google.com**") is used to provide a system to map domain names to IP addresses. It is essential because it allows us to easily access websites and other online services without remembering each website's IP address. -

Ethernet (Cat 6, Cat 7 cable) - a network cable used to connect computers and other devices to a network. It is the most common type of cable used in networking and is made up of four pairs of twisted copper wires. Category (**or Cat**) 6 and 7 cables are high-speed Ethernet cables that connect routers, switches, and other network devices. They are made up of four pairs of twisted copper wires and can support data transfer rates up to 10Gbps. The RJ45 connector is the most common type used in Ethernet cables. It is an 8-pin connector that looks like a wide telephone jack. It is used to connect the Ethernet cable to network devices.

Firewall - a system designed to prevent unauthorized access to or from a private network. It can be implemented as hardware, software, or both. Firewalls are essential because they can protect personal information and resources from malicious attacks such as viruses, worms, and hackers. They can also help to protect users from malicious websites, spam, and other unwanted content.

EXPLAIN IT TO ME: WIFI

Hotspot - a physical location where people can access a wireless local area network (WLAN) with the use of a router connected to an internet service provider. Hotspots are often found in public places such as airports, libraries, and coffee shops and allow users to access the internet for free or for a fee. It is also a feature on some cell phones that allows the device to act as a wireless router, allowing other devices to connect to the internet using the cellphone's 4G or 5G data connection.

IP v4 = (or **Internet Protocol Version 4**) is the fourth version of the Internet Protocol, the primary communication protocol used on the Internet. A connectionless protocol routes data packets between networks based on IP addresses. IP V4 is the most commonly used version of the internet protocol.

IP v6 = (or **Internet Protocol Version 6**) is the sixth version of the Internet Protocol, the primary communication protocol used on the Internet. A connectionless protocol routes data packets between networks based on IP addresses. IP V6 is the successor to IP V4 and provides a more extensive network address space and improved security features.

IEEE (or Institute of Electrical and Electronics Engineers) – is an international professional association that sets standards for technology, engineering, and computer science. IEEE is essential because its measures ensure the interoperability and safety of the latest technologies, and its publications provide a platform for researchers to share their findings.

Internet Service Provider (ISP) - a company that provides access to the internet. They offer internet connections via various technologies, including broadband, fiber, and satellite. They also provide web hosting, email, and other online services.

LAN (or Local Area Network) - a network of computers or devices connected in a limited area, such as a home, office, or school. It allows users to share printers, files, applications, and internet access. It is essential because it will enable users to collaborate and communicate with each other and with external networks. It also allows users to access the internet, printers, and applications.

Latency = the time it takes for data to travel from one point to another on the internet, usually measured in milliseconds. It is essential for applications like streaming video, online gaming, and voice-over IP (VoIP).

LIFI (or Li-Fi, and also Light Fidelity) - is a wireless communication technology that utilizes visible light or infrared light to transmit data wirelessly between devices. Unlike WIFI, which uses radio waves, LIFI modulates the intensity of LED (light-emitting diode) bulbs to encode data, which is then received by light-sensitive receivers.

EXPLAIN IT TO ME: WIFI

NIC (or **Network Interface Card**) - a computer hardware component (or can be an external USB dongle) that allows a computer to connect to a network. NICs are essential as they enable computers to communicate with each other, exchange data, and access resources, such as the internet.

Power over Ethernet (or **PoE**) - a technology that allows an access point to receive power over a standard Ethernet cable, rather than requiring a separate power cable. It is commonly used to power wireless access points, as it eliminates the need for a separate power source.

RJ-11 Connector - a modular connector used in telephone and data networking applications. It is a six-position, four-contact connector used mainly to connect a phone to a wall outlet. It is also connected to many other devices, including modems, fax machines, and other telecommunications equipment. The RJ-11 connector is typically mounted on the wall, and the telephone's line cord plugs into the wall outlet using the RJ-11 connector. The RJ-11 connector is similar in design to the larger RJ-45 connector but features only two rows of pins instead of eight.

RJ-45 Connector is an 8-pin modular connector used to connect Ethernet cables to networking devices. It is the most used type of connector for network cables and is also referred to as an 8P8C connector due to its eight pins and its position contacts. The RJ-45 connector is a physical interface for connecting cables to devices such as routers, switches, and modems. It is a type of registered jack designed to carry data signals on four twisted pairs of wires. The RJ-45 connector is available in various configurations, the most common being the T568A and T568B wiring configurations. The connector is typically used with Cat 5, Cat 5e, Cat 6 and Cat 7 cables and is designed to provide a secure, reliable connection between two devices.

Switch = a device that allows multiple devices to connect to a single network. It is essential because it can help manage and control the data flow on the web, allowing for increased speed, reliability, and security.

SSID (or **Service Set Identifier**) - a unique name assigned to a wireless network that identifies and distinguishes it from other wireless networks. It is essential because it allows authorized users to locate and connect to the correct network quickly.

WEP (or **Wired Equivalent Privacy**) - a security protocol used to protect a wireless network from unauthorized access. It was designed to provide the same level of security as a wired network, using encryption to scramble data transmitted over the airwaves. WEP encrypts data with a secret key shared between the access point (AP) and the clients. Each packet of data sent by the clients is encrypted with the private key and then sent to the access point; the AP decrypts the box using the same key. WEP also includes an authentication method that requires clients to enter a valid passphrase to access the wireless network. WEP is considered an outdated security protocol and is not recommended for modern wireless networks.

EXPLAIN IT TO ME: WIFI

WIFI (or **Wi-Fi**) - a wireless networking technology that enables devices to connect to a local area network (LAN) or the internet without requiring a physical connection.

WIFI 6 (or **WIFI 6E)** - the latest and current wireless standard that is also known as IEEE 802.11ax and 802.11ax. It provides better performance in congested areas and officially arrived in late 2019, and WIFI 6-enabled hardware is now the normal standard and brings faster connections, lower latency, and, for some devices, improved battery life. It also includes the WPA3 security protocol. WIFI 6E expands upon WIFI 6 by adding access to the 6 GHz spectrum.

WIFI 7 - also known as **802.11be**, is the next generation of WIFI technology designed to offer faster speeds, lower latency, and greater capacity compared to its predecessors. It operates on the 2.4 GHz, 5 GHz, and 6 GHz bands, supports wider 320 MHz channels, and introduces **Multi-Link Operation (MLO)** to use multiple frequency bands simultaneously for improved performance. Its goal is to provide up to 46 Gbps speeds, making it ideal for 8K streaming and virtual reality.

WPA, WPA2, or WPA3 – three of the most popular security protocols used to protect wireless networks. WPA, WPA2, and WPA3 encrypt data transmitted over the web, providing an extra layer of security and protecting the data from unauthorized access.

Virtual Private Network (or **VPN**) - a form of secure network connection (usually software-based) that allows users to access private networks over the internet. By using encryption and other security measures, a VPN provides a secure tunnel for data traffic between two or more computers, networks, or other devices. It can allow users to send data securely between two cities without risk of interception.

Voice over Internet Protocol (or **VoIP**), commonly abbreviated as VoIP, is a technology that enables the transmission of voice and multimedia content over the Internet Protocol (IP) networks. Instead of using traditional telephone lines, VoIP converts analog voice signals into digital data packets, which are then transmitted over IP-based networks, such as the internet or local area networks (LANs). VoIP allows users to make voice calls, video calls, and send multimedia messages using their internet connection, typically at a lower cost compared to traditional telephone services.

EXPLAIN IT TO ME: WIFI

25. Conclusion

In today's world, having a basic understanding of WIFI and how it can be leveraged for personal benefit is essential.

As more people travel frequently, it is evident that the world has come a long way since the days of dial-up internet. One of the significant advancements in technology that has made this possible is the introduction of WIFI and 5G cellular standards.

WIFI and 5G cellular standards have revolutionized how we stay connected, allowing us to access the internet, make phone calls, and share data from virtually anywhere. This has drastically improved how we communicate, making it easier to stay connected while you are on the go.

WIFI provides a connection to the internet without the need for wires or cables, allowing users to access the internet from almost anywhere. With WIFI, you can access the internet from virtually anywhere with a wireless connection, allowing you to stay connected while you are traveling or just out and about. 5G cellular standards provide even more freedom, allowing you to stay connected even when you are out of WIFI range. This means that you can access the internet and make phone calls virtually anywhere, even if no WIFI network is available.

Another benefit of WIFI and 5G cellular standards is the increased speed of the connection. WIFI connections are typically much faster than traditional dial-up connections, and 5G cellular standards can offer even faster speeds. This means you can access the internet faster, download files more quickly, and stream content faster than ever. The increased rates also mean you can access more data than ever. With WIFI and 5G cellular standards, you can access more websites, download more files, and stream more content without waiting for the connection to slow down.

This means you can stay connected and get more done while on the go. Finally, WIFI and 5G cellular standards provide increased security for your connection. WIFI connections use encryption to keep your data safe and secure, while 5G cellular standards use advanced security protocols to ensure that your data is not intercepted or stolen. This means you can access the internet without worrying about your data being compromised.

Overall, WIFI and 5G cellular standards have revolutionized how we stay connected, providing increased speed, data access, and security. This has drastically improved how we communicate and stay connected and has made it easier to access the internet and make phone calls on the go.

EXPLAIN IT TO ME: WIFI

This means that users can access the internet wherever they are without worrying about finding a place to plug in. This can be incredibly useful when traveling, as it eliminates the need to carry around a physical cable.

This is particularly useful for users who are on the go and need to access the internet quickly and easily. In addition to convenience and access, knowing WIFI and how it can be leveraged can also provide users with increased security.

WIFI networks are secure, meaning that only users who are authorized to access a particular network can do so. This provides an extra layer of security to users, as they can ensure their data is safe and secure. Finally, knowing what WIFI is and how it can be leveraged can provide users with the ability to save money.

Many WIFI networks are available for free or at a greatly reduced cost compared to normal traditional internet services. This can be incredibly beneficial for users who are on a budget and need to access the internet without breaking the bank.

Overall, knowing WIFI and how it can be leveraged is an essential skill for anyone who uses the internet. With WIFI, users can enjoy increased convenience, access to the internet in public places, increased security, and the potential to save money. By leveraging its potential, users can make the most of their internet experience.

EXPLAIN IT TO ME: WIFI

26. Credits

The author, at this moment, acknowledges the following credits –

Publication References

a.	Article on WIFI - https://en.wikipedia.org/wiki/Wi-Fi.
b.	Article by M. Gauthier, bandwidth - https://upload.wikimedia.org/wikipedia/commons/.
c.	Article by J. Kastrenakes (3 Oct 2018), The Verge WI-FI now has version numbers.
d.	Article on https://www.howtogeek.com/188235/how-to-set-up-a-wireless-network-in-your-home/.
e.	Article on HowStuffWorks - https://computer.howstuffworks.com/wireless-network.htm.
f.	Article on WIFI Technology by FireFly Networks - https://www.fireflynetworks.co.in/blog/wifi-technology.
g.	IEEE Xplore - "IEEE 802.15.7-2018 - IEEE Standard for Local and metropolitan area networks--Part 15.7: Short-Range Wireless Optical Communication Using Visible Light" - IEEE Standards Association.

Image References

h.	Photo on Cover by Rohit Chouda on Unsplash.
i.	Photos with Light Blue backgrounds were purchased on VectorStock.
j.	Photo on Mesh Networks by Alina Grubnya on Unsplash.
k.	Photos on Modems, Routers & Switches attributed to AT&T, Netgear were taken by author.
l.	Photo on Access point by Ubiquiti Networks.
m.	Photo on wet WIFI symbol by Jadon Kelly on Unsplash.
n.	Photo on Access point by Compare-Fibre on Unsplash.
o.	Photo on Speedtest by Mika Baumels on Unsplash.
p.	Photo on RJ45 connections by Thomas Jense on Unsplash.
q.	Photo on TV and streaming by Julian O. Haydon on Unsplash.
r.	The ® WIFI symbol mark and logos are registered trademarks owned by the Wi-Fi Alliance, Inc.

EXPLAIN IT TO ME: WIFI

27. Notes

All Covers & Illustrations have been designed and implemented by the author.

www.ingramcontent.com/pod-product-compliance
Lightning Source LLC
Chambersburg PA
CBHW051926210526
45473CB00006B/2156